From Barter to Bills

to Bills

The History of Paper Money

By F. R. Robinson

Celebration Press
Pearson Learning Group

Contents

Does Paper Money Make Cents?

Think about that
$1 bill in your wallet.
What can you buy
with it? Could you
buy juice to go with
your lunch? Would
there be enough to
buy dessert?

What about the bill
itself? It's just a piece
of paper with some
writing and fancy decorations on it. So why does it
have value? Why can you give that piece of paper to
someone in the cafeteria and get $1 worth of
macaroni and cheese? If you handed the cashier a
different piece of paper—say one from your
notebook—all you'd get is a strange look!

The value of coins makes more sense. You can
imagine that the copper and zinc your pennies are
made from might be worth something. But what
about paper? Who decided it should have value?
What's the story?

The Days Before Money

Long ago, people didn't have money. They didn't need it. They hunted and gathered their food, and they made their own shelters and clothing. Doing all of these tasks kept people quite busy, and they didn't need much more than what they could make or find themselves.

Over time, people learned to raise their own animals instead of hunting. They learned to grow vegetables and fruits instead of searching for them in the fields and forests. People also figured out they could trade things with one another. If they had extra potatoes but no cows, they might go to a neighbor who had many cows but no potatoes. Then the two would try to agree on how many potatoes a cow was worth and make a trade.

This system of trade is called **barter**, and it has worked for many people in various places. In some parts of the world it still does.

But as people began to live in bigger groups, their wants and needs grew. So did their skills. People learned to make cloth, pots, utensils, and tools. The barter system still worked, but things got more complicated. What if someone who made cloth wanted a pot, but the person who made pots didn't want cloth—he wanted a cow? What could they do?

Soon people began to use objects that had value in and of themselves for trading. For example, people living in coastal areas began using rare and beautiful shells, which were desired as ornaments. The shells were considered valuable, and people traded them for what they needed.

Cowrie shells and glass beads are among the items once used as money.

The Chinese used brightly-colored, glossy shells as money about 3,500 years ago. In other places, people used blocks of salt, beads, whale teeth, and even stones. This system worked best for people who lived near one another. In order to make it work, they had to agree on the value of the item used as money.

There was one item that most people agreed was valuable—metal. Metal could be used to make things, it was shiny and pretty, and it was hard to find. Gold was especially valuable because it was so scarce and beautiful. In many places, people were happy to trade their pots or cows for it.

But how many lumps of gold was a cow worth? How many chunks of silver equaled one pot? Someone had to decide. People started weighing the metal at each exchange. A certain weight was agreed upon to be worth a certain amount.

Coins to the Rescue!

Then about 640 B.C. in Lydia, a kingdom in what is now Turkey, people had a better idea. They took a mixture of silver and gold and formed it into small oval-shaped lumps. They marked

A Lydian gold coin from around 550 B.C.

each one to tell how much it weighed and how pure it was. Each lump was stamped with a design, showing that the king guaranteed its value. The people trusted the new money because they trusted their king. They traded these metal lumps for things they wanted. Whoever owned the metal lumps knew exactly what they were worth. These were the first coins.

Soon coins showed up in many parts of the world and became very popular. But while coins solved many problems, they also created a few. As people traveled farther to buy and sell goods, it became difficult to carry the money they needed. Bags of metal coins were heavy.

Bags of coins were hard to hide, too. Bandits and other dishonest people found ways to steal them. Other thieves clipped a tiny bit of metal off the edge of each coin—so little that it was hardly noticeable. They collected the clippings until they had enough to sell or melt down to make their own coins. Coin makers themselves sometimes used cheaper, less pure metals to make coins. They saved the pure metals for themselves.

All these practices were unfair, dishonest, and troublesome. Although coins had their advantages and still do, there had to be something better. But as it turned out, a new and better form of money would not be developed until the invention of a new material—paper.

Some ancient Chinese and Roman coins

Paying With Paper

Before paper was invented, people used **papyrus**, made from stems of the papyrus plant, to write on as well as **parchment**, or dried sheepskin. But these surfaces were unevenly shaped and thick.

Early Chinese paper money

Paper was invented by the Chinese about A.D. 105. It was light and could be cut to any size. Within a few hundred years, the Chinese realized they could make paper money. Other people had paper by then, but no one else had thought of using it for this purpose.

A famous explorer from Venice named Marco Polo visited China about 1300. He was amazed when he saw paper money in use. In his journals he described how the paper was cut, stamped with a value, and used to buy things. Marco Polo told the Europeans about the use of paper money, but they didn't trust the idea. They couldn't see how paper, which cost very little, could be valuable.

In the meantime, written promises to pay a specific debt had been around for hundreds of years. (Today these are called **IOU**s, which stands for "I owe you.") These were somewhat like paper money, but they were just agreements between individuals.

For example, suppose Trader A owed Trader B ten apples for a bushel of corn. Trader A might give Trader B an IOU. That piece of paper had value to Trader B, who knew he could eventually get ten apples for it. That type of exchange was a step toward the use of paper money.

Banks, which came into existence when money did, provided a safe place to keep it. In 1661 the Stockholm Bank in Sweden issued a "note" to a customer who deposited a certain amount of metal. The use of this kind of note, called a bank note, developed from the use of private paper notes. Bank notes could be carried around much more easily than coins and could be used to buy goods. The owner of the note could always go to the bank and get the specified amount of metal.

This system worked for about a year. But people were afraid foreigners would collect the bank notes and then cash them in for a lot of the country's gold, thus draining the country's wealth. Soon these bank notes were no longer made.

Paper Money Comes to America

Some of the first paper money in North America was made from playing cards. In 1685, France ruled Canada, and soldiers were paid with money shipped from France. Once, when shipments were delayed at sea, the soldiers grew angry. In an attempt to keep them happy, the governor had his officials gather

Playing-card money

up playing cards, which were plentiful. The cards were marked with specific values, and official seals and signatures were added. These cards were later known as **promissory notes**. They represented a promise to pay the amount indicated on the card when the shipment of money came in.

Meanwhile American colonists were using foreign coins as well as barter. The coins were brought over and spent by visiting Europeans. The colonists then used the coins to buy European goods. The merchants took their earnings back to Europe, so the colonists' supply of coins didn't grow.

In 1652 the Massachusetts Bay Colony decided to build a factory to make official coins. Other colonies followed. Soon there were coins with different values from the various colonies. Then, in 1690, Massachusetts issued paper money, too. All these different kinds of money were confusing!

In 1775 the American Revolution against the British broke out because the British passed unfair laws and taxes and tried to control trade in the colonies. In 1776 the thirteen colonies declared independence and joined to become the United States of America. The Continental Congress printed paper bills, called **continentals**, to pay for the war. The bills were backed only by the new government's plan to collect tax money, which it was not given the power to do, so people didn't trust these bills, and they didn't use them. A continental became almost worthless.

The United States won the war in 1783. In 1792 the first national money system was set up, with the dollar as the basic unit. The colonists knew about dollar coins from European countries, especially the Spanish pieces of eight, which were called dollars. Only the government could coin money and regulate its value. It issued no paper money until 1861, only coins.

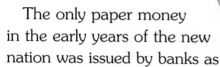

Many colonial bank notes had intricate designs.

The only paper money in the early years of the new nation was issued by banks as bank notes. The banks promised to exchange their bank notes for gold or silver coins at any time the customer wished. But the banks weren't always well run or honest. They didn't always have enough gold or silver to back up the paper money. Paper money lost its value and the people's trust—again.

Counterfeiting—making fake money—was another problem. There were thousands of different kinds of bank notes with different designs. It was rather easy for counterfeiters to get away with copying the already confusing bank notes. People didn't always know what the real notes looked like.

To trip up the counterfeiters, banks made their notes more complicated. They used secret printing marks, more detailed designs, and portraits etched by the finest artists, which would be harder to copy. But the counterfeiters just got more skillful.

Greenbacks

At the start of the Civil War in 1861, the United States money system was a mess. Coins were again scarce, counterfeiting was common, and banks often failed. To put everything in order and to help pay for the cost of the Civil War, Congress authorized the U.S. Treasury to issue paper money. The United States notes printed in 1862 were called **greenbacks** because their backs were printed in green.

These notes could not be exchanged for gold or silver, but they were **legal tender**, money declared by law to be acceptable as payment for debts. This time, people used the money because they trusted the government. Even when the government announced in 1879 that the greenbacks still in circulation could be exchanged for gold, people did not rush to turn them in.

In the meantime, in 1863 and 1864 the government had set up a system of privately owned banks. These banks issued national bank notes, which became the nation's main currency.

At first, paper money was printed in the basement of the Treasury Building in Washington, D.C. Just six people had the job of cutting apart the sheets of money that came off the printing presses. Today, instead of six, about 2,500 people work to make U.S. paper money. Bills are made in two different buildings in Washington, D.C., and in a new one in Fort Worth, Texas.

Over the years the United States went on and off the **gold standard** several times before abandoning it in 1971. This means that the government will no longer exchange paper money for gold. However, a dollar bill still has value because people have trust in the government and its stability. It controls vast wealth and resources, and they believe it can continue to collect taxes and govern.

A government employee straightens sheets of money coming off the press in Washington, D.C.

The Design of Paper Money

Take a close look at a one-dollar bill. Complicated, isn't it? Words, numbers, letters, and detailed pictures almost cover the paper. What do all these features mean? Let's look first at the face, or front, of the bill.

Serial number
Every bill has its own number, called the serial number.

Signatures People signed the earliest paper money to make it official. Signatures still appear on bills for the same reason. Of course, they are printed now, not handwritten. There are two signatures on each bill—one of the Treasurer of the United States and the other of the Secretary of the Treasury.

Portrait A picture of George Washington appears in the center of a dollar bill. The name of the person in the portrait is written below it. Why do you think George Washington was chosen for this bill?

The country's name "The United States of America" appears on the front and back of each bill.

Laurel leaves The leaves along the bottom of the portrait and on the right and left sides of the bill are laurel leaves. Laurel is the ancient Greek symbol for victory.

Seals On the left the dollar bill has the seal of the Federal Reserve Bank from which the bill came. On the right is the official seal of the Treasury, printed in green ink over the number "ONE," printed in black. This is very hard to counterfeit.

The number one The number one is written both as a numeral and spelled out. It appears 6 times on the face and 10 times on the back.

Federal Reserve number The number that identifies the Federal Reserve District appears four times on the front. (See page 20.)

Now look at the back of the dollar bill.

National Motto "In God We Trust" appears in the center of the bill above the "ONE."

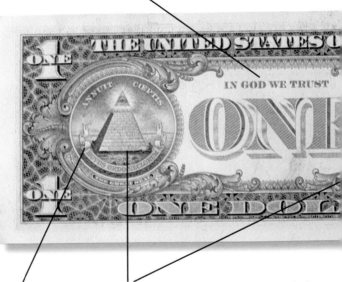

The Great Seal of the United States Both the face and reverse, or back, of this seal are shown.

The reverse of the seal is on the left of the bill. The pyramid, with 13 steps, is a symbol of strength and permanence. It's not complete, which symbolizes future growth for the United States. *Annuit Coeptis* is a Latin motto that means "God has smiled on our undertakings." The eye above the pyramid represents the eye of God. *Novus Ordo Seclorum* means "a new order of the ages."

The Paper The paper, made of cotton and linen, is specially manufactured for money only. Look at a real bill to see the tiny red and blue threads in it. These threads are embedded in the paper through a secret process, to prevent counterfeiting.

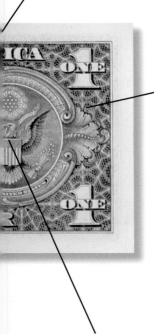

Border Notice how complicated the design is. Produced by a special machine, the fine lines and scrollwork are almost impossible to copy.

A bald eagle, the national bird, appears on the face of the Great Seal, which is on the right side of the bill. In its talons it holds an olive branch, which symbolizes peace, and 13 arrows. These arrows symbolize the colonies' fight for liberty. There are 13 stars above the eagle. The Latin phrase *E Pluribus Unum* means "out of many, one"—one country from many people, and has 13 letters. The shield on the eagle's chest has 13 stripes. Why all the thirteens? That's the number of original colonies or states.

The Federal Reserve System was created by Congress in 1913 to be the nation's central bank and to control its money supply. Nicknamed the Fed, it is made up of 12 Federal Reserve Banks located in major cities inside the 12 Federal Reserve districts. Each bank has a letter assigned to it as well as a number. The following chart will help you determine which Federal Reserve Bank a particular bill comes from. Look for the letter of the bank located inside the bank's seal on the face of the dollar bill.

City and State	Letter	District Number
Boston, Massachusetts	A	1
New York, New York	B	2
Philadelphia, Pennsylvania	C	3
Cleveland, Ohio	D	4
Richmond, Virginia	E	5
Atlanta, Georgia	F	6
Chicago, Illinois	G	7
St. Louis, Missouri	H	8
Minneapolis, Minnesota	I	9
Kansas City, Missouri	J	10
Dallas, Texas	K	11
San Francisco, California	L	12

Paper Money Today

The government now designs and prints $1, $2, $5, $10, $20, $50, and $100 bills. Each bill has a different portrait, as well as different borders and designs. George Washington is on the $1 bill, Thomas Jefferson on the $2 bill, Abraham Lincoln on the $5 bill, Alexander Hamilton on the $10 bill, Andrew Jackson on the $20 bill, Ulysses S. Grant on the $50 bill, and Benjamin Franklin on the $100 bill.

Bills larger than $100 have not been printed since 1946 because people didn't use them. They realized that it was safer to carry and use checks for large amounts of money. Before that time there was even a $100,000 bill! But it was used only for transactions between Federal Reserve Banks.

A newly designed $10 bill (top) and an earlier bill

Today's bills also contain features to prevent counterfeiting. Counterfeiters once had to be excellent artists because they had to copy the designs from bills in precise detail by hand. Today photocopiers, computers, scanners, and new printing methods have added to the ways counterfeiters can copy money and try to pass it as real.

Fortunately ways to prevent counterfeiting have also been improved. The paper, the designs, and even the inks are chosen to make money especially hard to copy. Counterfeiting is a very serious crime. Counterfeiters are almost always caught and spend years in jail for their crimes.

Even though the amount of counterfeit money in circulation is small, counterfeiting is still a problem. To address the problem, in the early 1990s the government set up a council to study ways to make money safer. To study the money, they used about $500,000 (half a million dollars) in real bills! Research teams tested how durable the bills were by crumpling, folding, and washing them. They soaked them in gasoline, acids, and laundry soaps. The researchers themselves made copies of bills to try to find ways to make counterfeiting more difficult.

The word *ten* appears in microprinting on the numeral on a $10 bill.

The changes recommended by the council took effect in stages between 1996 and 2000. All the bills were changed except the $1 and $2 bills. However, the size, basic colors, people pictured, and national symbols remain the same.

The most obvious change is in the size of the portrait, which has been enlarged and moved slightly to the left. Other new features are not so easy to spot, however. For example, all new bills include special hidden security threads that show the letters *USA*, the **denomination** of the bill, and a flag on certain bills. They also glow special colors when placed under ultraviolet light. **Microprinting**, readable only with a magnifier, appears in special places on each type of bill.

Take a look at an older $5 or $10 bill and a new one. What other changes do you notice? A watermark, a design created in the paper-making process, shows the same portrait that's on the bill, but you can see it only when you hold the bill up to a light. On the background of the portrait are fine-line printing patterns, which are hard to copy. All these new features help make sure that the bills in your wallet are genuine.

So think about that dollar bill you're about to spend. It is more than a piece of paper. It's worth 100 pennies, 10 dimes, 4 quarters, or whatever you can buy with it. It carries part of our history and took thousands of years to get here. So use it well. It's earned its value!

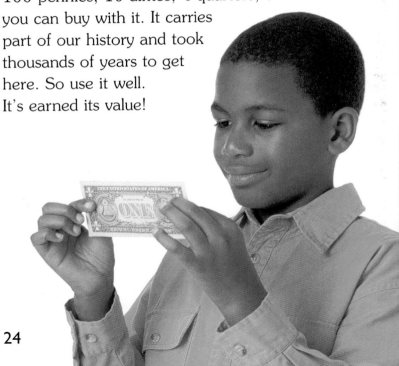